Dying to Live in the Eternal
Moment of Now

By

Pastor David G. Garty

Dying To Live in the Eternal Moment of Now
By Pastor David G. Garty

ISBN-10: 0-9742432-8-0
ISBN-13: 978-0-9742432-8-3

Flying Scroll Publishing, LLC.
P.O. Box 246
Fort Atkinson, WI 53538
www.flyingscrollpublishing.com

I'd like to dedicate this book to all those who still carry the pains, hurts and hang-ups of their past... that they may discover their true freedom as they enter into their position and identity in their Savior and Lord Jesus Christ.

ACKNOWLEDGEMENTS

Much appreciation and gratitude are to be given to all of those who have embraced me and encouraged me in my walk with Christ. There are numerous individuals and persons who come to mind but I would like to say a special thanks to my wife, Lin, who has been my greatest support and encouragement on this journey, and to my three sons.

I would like to state my gratitude and appreciation to Terrie Knox who is my editor, without whose help and encouragement this would not be put together.

My appreciation also goes to Walt Cueto. He was able to put the cover art together from the description I gave him of my vision.

But most of all, my thanks and praise go to my Lord and Savior Jesus Christ who has truly walked and talked with me through this journey. May He be glorified and lifted up in the lives of all those who will be encouraged and changed through this book.

Contents

INTRODUCTION

The thoughts and the expressions that are found in this book come from a journey of discovering who I really am in Christ. My life journey included pain, hurts and hang-ups that I began to experience at a young age. I did not grow up in a Christian home but what we would describe in today's terms as a dysfunctional family. I'm not even sure 'dysfunctional' was a term back then. Much of what I experienced was considered normal in many families.

My home life was filled with sexual abuse, drugs, alcohol, witchcraft and strife. It seemed as if my father and my step-mother were always in competition with each other competing to see whose way would prevail. There was tremendous physical abuse that they demonstrated towards each other which found its way into my life and the lives of my brothers and sister. I can't speak for my siblings. I don't know what they were experiencing or feeling about all that was happening. I can only speak from my perspective based upon the fears and the hurts that I carried within my own life.

When I was about 8 years old, I remember helping a friend deliver Sunday morning newspapers. We had gotten up early that morning, about 6 am. After we had finished his paper route, as we were heading back to our homes, he had asked me to go to church with him. I had never been to church before and I was looking forward to seeing what it was all about.

The events that happened that day are among those I will never forget. When I came into the house after our route, I had asked my parents if I could go to church with my friend. My father spoke up very quickly and said I could. But my stepmother became very angry and stated that I could not. This created an instant and very aggressive fight between my parents, a fight which I didn't understand... simply because I asked if I could go to church. My father insisted that I go and my stepmother fought against me going. Amidst it all, my dad told me to go get dressed. My stepmother became so angry that she began to physically attack me, hitting me in the face with her fist. My father stepped in to stop her and told me to go.

As I left, my friend met me in front of the house. I was crying and bleeding from my lips and nose. I told him I didn't want to go to church like this, but he insisted that I go with him. As we reached the church, I again told him I did not want to go in. He left me and went in to get his mother and father. They and some others came out to talk to me. They began to clean my face and wiped the blood away. It was there that I began to sense something about those people that was different.

After that experience, I discovered the reason my parents had fought about me going to church. My stepmother had a high school class reunion that Sunday afternoon and my father did not want to go because he didn't want to meet or be around some of her male friends that she went to school with. My asking to go to church became his excuse to stay home.

A few weeks later my friend's father came over and invited our whole family to come to church. I went to church regularly after that and my brothers and sister were also encouraged to go. It was through this experience that my love for the Lord began.

About this time I was introduced to Jesus Christ and was taught that He could resolve our troubles and difficulties. As I continued to go to church and to grow in my understanding of the Word, I became confused and frustrated. Many of those who would encourage me in the church would invite me to play with their children on the weekends. As I spent time in their homes, I discovered that some of their lives didn't seem much different than mine. I began to question whether the work of Christ was truly able to set anyone free from the pain, the hurts and the hang ups that I so dearly wanted to escape.

But yet there was something that was different. Even when there was arguing, yelling, and frustrations in the homes with Christ, there was a love that seemed to overshadow it all. It gave me hope that there really was something more, that the Bible was not exaggerating. I didn't want to simply walk in the truth, I wanted to truly know it, to truly experience the power of it. I wanted to know how one could overcome the pain from sexual abuse, overcome the wounds of physical abuse, and overcome the hang-ups from mental abuse.

So this book is about a life search that the Lord has led me through as I sought the answers to the many questions I had. Through the encouragement and help of others who also hungered for a freedom from their hurts, pains and hang-ups that they were not fully experiencing, I have discovered the true freedom that Jesus said was ours. When we know the truth, the truth will set us free.

Chapter 1

DYING TO LIVE

There are many wonderful individuals serving within Christian Ministries who desire to see people set free from the hurts, pains, and hang-ups that they struggle with. Yet, as I study and listen to many different ideas on helping and encouraging these individuals, I do not see many people approaching the problems of an individual from the Biblical view of man's troubles or 'fall.'

It seems to me that the idea of focusing on the self-esteem of an individual focuses on the outside of the person, on his or her earth suit. It is a person's self-worth which speaks about who they are on the inside. Isn't self-esteem about one's pride, egotism, conceit and vanity? The Bible teaches death to self and life in Christ. Yet, how can one have full life in Christ if they try to keep alive what Christ crucified?

I have set out on a journey to discover why so many Christians are unable to overcome the habitual patterns or behaviors that have been defeated in the works of Christ Jesus on the cross. Is there something that we have failed to teach and encourage those coming to Christ? Is there something that we are not teaching? Are we teaching all of the truth or just a part of the truth? Are we telling each one who comes to Christ what it will cost them? Are we afraid we'll lose them when we tell them that life is no longer about them, but about Christ and Him alone? This book is written not only through my own struggles, but also from the struggles of many fellow believers. Together we have spent time working through this battle that seems to shipwreck so many as they follow Christ.

A thought to reflect upon throughout this book will be, "Dying to live in the eternal moment of now." We need to die to ourselves so that the life of Christ can live through us. My heart's purpose is to show that for each individual believer to grow to maturity, they must grow through their understanding of who they are in Christ Jesus and who He is in them. As a Pastor, I do not believe these are the same.

Who the believer is in Christ speaks of the believer's position and who Christ is in the believer speaks of the believer's identity in the world. Position and identity are two distinct truths of the believer's relationship to Christ. One without the other will leave believers struggling in their difficulties which will hound them in everything they do in their spiritual journey.

The Apostle Paul stated in Romans 6, "Or do you not know that all of us who have been baptized into Christ Jesus have been baptized into His death." The verses go on to say, "Knowing this, that our old self was crucified with Him, that our body of sin might be done away with, that we should no longer be slaves to sin; for he who has died is freed from sin."

It is the belief of this Pastor that much of the counseling and materials written are not about setting people free as much as they are about making a gain from the hurts, pains, and hang-ups of those for whom Christ died. I know that this sounds like a bold statement. I know this is not true for all. But the Apostle

Paul and the Apostle Peter said this would be true in the last days.

The Apostle Peter wrote in II Peter 2, "Many will follow their sensuality, and because of them the way of the truth will be maligned; and in their greed they will exploit you with false words." Today this scripture is exemplified when it's all about money; when people use the gospel for selfish gain. It's about pride, egotism, conceit, and vanity, "always learning and never able to come to the knowledge of the truth." (II Timothy 3:7)

It is the heart of Christ Jesus that all men would find themselves free from the hurts, pains, and hang-ups that so entangle their lives. However, this freedom comes only when they are free from themselves and their self-centeredness. Life is really not about self-esteem but about self-worth and value. Again, there is a distinct difference in these two terms. One represents the temporal, material world and all it holds; while the other represents the eternal realm and all that it holds.

These two words represent two kinds of lives. One is a life of self-centeredness and the other is a life of selflessness. One seeks to gain everything it can, because it believes happiness is found in what one can have and can do for one's self. The other seeks to give away or lose itself, for in giving its self, it finds true happiness and true life. In Luke 9 verse 23 Jesus said, "If anyone wishes to follow Me, he must deny himself, and take up his cross daily and follow Me." This declaration is not about keeping one's self-esteem alive. It is about putting it to death, for if we don't, we will lose our life in the end for all eternity as stated in verse 24. "For whoever wishes to save his life will lose it, but whoever loses his life for My sake, he is the one who will save it."

Chapter 2

GETTING REAL

One of the first steps in getting real is to help people discover the core reason or reasons for the frustration and struggles that are entangling their lives. The Hebrew writer has written in the first verse of chapter 12, "Let us also lay aside every encumbrance, and the sin which so easily entangles us."

To help someone see their encumbrance or entanglement, we must begin where the Bible begins. Our troubles all started in the garden with Adam and Eve believing they could be like God and know everything that God knows. (Genesis 3:1-24) It is here that most of our struggles or problems can be found; it is when we are playing God.

This may seem hard and sound like a strong statement, but in actuality, it really shouldn't. What was it that Satan said to Eve in the garden? When he found Eve there in the garden by herself, he didn't say, 'If you eat this fruit you'll be just like me, the devil.' Nor did he say, 'If you eat this fruit you'll be evil.' When the devil speaks, he never says what he means. He always distorts truth because a lie is always about getting someone to believe an exaggeration that covers the truth. Satan said to Eve, "If you eat this fruit that God told you not to eat, you'll be like God." The root of all our hurts, pains, and hang-ups are found right there in the garden. The oldest temptation and the oldest struggle for man is that he is still trying to play God.

Here is the beginning of all our troubles. It is when we call our own shots and start making our own rules. As we start making our own rules, we start placing ourselves at the top of the world. It's not just about controlling our own lives. We want to control everyone else around us as well. How many times have we thought that we know better than those around us, especially thinking we know better than those with authority over us? How many times have we thought that we've known better for others than they themselves did? And, if they did what we said, it would surely go better for them, but especially better for us. Yet, many of us fail to recognize all the problems that we are still having. Our playing God is hard work. That is why we fail at it, for we were never created to be God.

This past summer, our oldest son David received some material in the mail on how to take complete control of your life by becoming a "Neo Tech Person." This material illustrates the point being made here. The following was found in some of the material:

"Dear friend, this may be the luckiest day of your life. You are one of only a few selected people to receive this personal memo. You're going to have prosperity in every area of your life-emotionally, romantically, financially, personally. You'll learn how to control anyone and make any man or woman like you, admire you and love you. Thirty days after you receive this kit you will be doing this and much more. GUARANTEED!

1. *Guaranteed: Regardless of physical appearance you can have sexual relationships with beautiful women of your choice in one week or less.*
2. *You will be such a superior lover that those women will fall in love with you and want to be yours forever.*
3. *You will be making thousands of dollars each week at first and each day eventually. Guaranteed!*
4. *You will get rid of all physical illness, all physical incompetence, pains, allergies and addictions.*
5. *You will lose all your fat. Guaranteed!*
6. *You will become very smart quickly, and when you talk everyone will listen.*
7. *Beautiful women and powerful men will almost beg to be your friends.*
8. *You will get an instant promotion.*

So you see, it's almost magical and mystical from this special power called Neo Tech, even an ordinary person, even a first rate nerd like I was, evolved into something with a super human life, the life of the god-man. I spent the past four years writing it all down, step by step, the secret power just as it lifted me from nerd to god-man who can take as much sex, power and money as you want from life. Receive my 458 turn-key manual called god-man: our final evolution."

The problem with this kind of stuff is that people read it and believe it and then buy it all because they are hurting, full of pain, and have all kinds of hang-ups. Deep down inside of us, we want to be God. We want to control it all. Yet, who of us would openly admit, 'I want to be God?' Not only is this a problem in the world, it is still a problem for many in the Church as well.

Every day of our lives, we make choices that imply we're smarter than God, that we're wiser than God. We willfully disobey God and say that we're going to do what we think is best. This is playing God.

We still are playing lord of the ring, the ring being the sphere in which everything about us is like we want it to be and done how we want it to be done. It's about making us feel good and being comfortable.

The Bible is not a book that is based on feeling good and being comfortable. Although it is not wrong to feel good or to be comfortable, the real issue is about being obedient to God.

Chapter 3

WHERE TO START

When leading a person to Jesus Christ, whether he is a believer or not, we need to start right at the beginning. Coming to Christ is not just about our sins being forgiven. It's about a total change in our thought life, our attitudes, our choice of words, and our way of behaving. II Corinthians 5:17 says, "Therefore if anyone is in Christ, he is a new creature; the old things passed away; behold, new things have come."

First, let's note where the person is in this verse: it says that he is "in Christ." Much of the church has failed at teaching the true position of where a believer is when they first come to Christ. There has been much focus on Christ in the believer, but little of the believer in Christ. It is the believer's position in Christ that brings full victory and abundant living.

When we teach only Christ in us, we are encouraging the believer to maintain full control over his life. He still tells God what he wants God to do for him and how he would like it done. I know that there are those who will say, but the Bible says, "Greater is He who is in you than he who is in the world." (I John 4:4) They will also quote Philippians 4:13, "I can do all things through Him who strengthens me." Let me ask a question here. Why is it that we are seeing and watching so many believers who are taught these verses yet still struggling with sin? The answer again lies in one's position in Christ, not in one's ability to control one's own life.

Jesus teaches us this truth in John 15 when speaking of the vine and the branches. Listen to His words: "I am the true vine, and My Father is the vine-dresser. Every branch in Me that does not bear fruit, He takes away; and every branch that bears fruit, He prunes it, that it may bear more fruit. You are already clean because of the word which I have spoken to you. Abide in Me, and I in you. As the branch cannot bear fruit of itself, unless it abides in the vine, so neither can you, unless you abide in Me. I am the vine, you are the branches; he who abides in Me, and I in him, he bears much fruit; for apart from Me you can do nothing." [KEY VERSE HERE: LISTEN] "If anyone does not abide in Me, he is thrown away as a branch, and dries up; and they gather them, and cast them into the fire, and they are burned. If you abide in Me, and My words abide in you, ask whatever you wish, and it shall be done for you." (John 15 1-7)

Here again we find that the believer's position is always in abiding, not in being strong. For outside of Christ there is no power for living this Christian life. Strength only comes from our position in Him. In this passage of scripture we find eight different times where the scripture refers to abiding in Him. Not to abide in Him would be a bad situation for the believer. The branch is supported by the vine and not the vine by its branches. There is no life or fruit outside of the vine.

Just look around and be honest with yourself. I deal with and counsel many who are believers in Christ and yet they experience neither power nor the abundant life that is promised by Christ. We are working with many in our marriage counseling who are ready to walk away from their marriages. They state they are tired of trying. When we begin to talk about their experience with Christ, they acknowledge that Christ is in their life. However, there just hasn't been any real change in their attitudes and behaviors. This often flows out of a lack of teaching or no teaching on their position in Christ. When we begin to share about their position in Christ, they begin to ask why no one has shared this truth before or how is it that no one is telling the full truth. So, let's look at our position in Christ and discover our power and our authority.

Chapter 4

KNOWING OUR POSITION

It all starts again with Christ Jesus. In His death, the Bible teaches that we were in Him and died with Him. When we look to the Bible, we'll find that it says in Colossians 3:3-4, "For you have died and your life is hidden with Christ in God. When Christ, who is our life, is revealed, then you also will be revealed with Him in glory."

First, let's note that it says, "you have died." Next, it says that you are "hidden with Christ in God". Do you know why one is hidden with Christ? It is because outside of Christ there is no life. The Bible clearly states that we are dead, hidden with Christ. But, let me ask another question. Where is Christ? Here again it says that "I am hidden with Christ in God." Christ is in the Father as I am in Christ. To live outside of my position is to live in death.

Listen to verse 4 of chapter 3, "When Christ, who is our life, is revealed, then you also will be revealed with Him in glory." Verse four clearly states that Christ is my life, therefore He is my identity. So, as a true believer, I can honestly say, 'My life is Jesus' life', for without Him there is no life.

Watch what else the verse says about me. It goes on to say that when Christ is revealed, then I also will be revealed with Him in glory. So, let's ask another question. Where am I in the meantime? Again, the scripture says so clearly that I am hidden and I need to remain hidden until Christ returns. I am not to leave my hiding place until Christ returns in glory. In other words, I am not going to leave my position in Christ. I am to let Jesus live out His life in and through this temple which is my body.

I am a spiritual being hidden in Christ while living in a temporary tent... an earth suit. This is why I can do what the scripture says in verses 5-17 of Colossians

27

chapter 3. Life is no longer about me and fulfilling my desires. Life is about obedience and fulfilling the desires and will of Christ Jesus. Just as Jesus lived to fulfill the will of the Father, so now do I live to fulfill the will of my Lord and Savior.

One of the disciples asked Jesus to show them the Father. Jesus said to him, "Have I been so long with you, and yet you have not come to know Me, Phillip? He who has seen Me has seen the Father; how do you say, 'Show us the Father?' Do you not believe that I am in the Father, and the Father is in Me? The words that I say to you I do not speak on My own initiative, but the Father abiding in Me does His works." (John 14:8-10)

Jesus' living was so that the Father might be heard and seen in and through His life. It was the heart of Jesus to show the world the Father by laying down His "equality with the Father and emptying Himself, taking the form of a bond servant, and being made in the likeness of men. And being found in appearance as a man, He humbled Himself by becoming obedient to the point of death, even death on a cross." (Philippians 2:5-8)

Here again is the heart of man's troubles. It's about whom you are living for. Are you living for yourself or for the One who made you? It really doesn't take long for one to discover the answer. For me it was in 1987 when the Lord started to teach me what it is to die. I was no longer serving as a Pastor. I had entered the insurance world which I did not enjoy. I was trying the best that I could to provide an income for my family. It was for a time and a season. The Lord used this time to grow me up in Him.

In one of my morning study times with the Lord, I was reading and writing on the book of Philippians. My study that particular morning was in chapter 2. When I came to verses 3-8 and had read through them, I found myself troubled. My heart started to hurt and I sensed the Spirit of God saying, 'this is what you need to do with your family.' I told the Lord that I didn't know how to do what was being asked in these verses. I told Him that if He wanted me to learn what these verses meant then He would have to teach me. I found myself turning this passage of scripture into my prayer for the next seven years. It was almost the only thing that I prayed for those seven years. It wasn't that I was a slow learner, but God was working in my family as well.

Let's look at Philippians 2:3-8. It is written, "Do nothing from selfishness or empty conceit, but with humility of mind let each of you regard one another as more important than himself; do not merely look out for your own personal interests, but also for the interests of others. Have this attitude in yourselves which was also in Christ Jesus, who although He existed in the form of God, did not regard equality with God a thing to be grasped, but emptied Himself, taking the form of a bond servant, and being made in the likeness of men. And being found in appearance as a man, He humbled Himself by becoming obedient to the point of death, even death on a cross."

In this passage of scripture we can pull out and find the answer to all of man's troubles. Before I go any further there are two more verses from this second chapter in Philippians that I must share with you. These are verses 20 and 21: "For I have no one else of kindred spirit who will genuinely be concerned for your welfare. For they all seek after their own interests, not those of Christ Jesus."

These are life changing verses for any and all who would dare to put them into practice. I first asked myself and the Lord, How does anyone do nothing from selfishness or empty conceit? What does it really mean to have a mind of humility and regard someone else as more important than yourself? I don't mind looking out for someone else's interest but to put their interest ahead of mine; what's that all about? Not only did I find myself with these questions, but also I was troubled by verses 20 and 21. You see, I loved pastoring and I loved speaking and teaching the Word of God. It was my life! Maybe that is why I didn't enjoy the insurance business even though God used it to teach me how to truly serve others.

These two verses also caused a disturbing question for me: Whose interest was I serving in the Church? I truly believe that many serving in the Church, well-meaning as they are, are serving out of personal interest, not the interest of Christ Jesus. Was I speaking and teaching and serving because I was being heard and seen and well thought of? Or was I allowing Christ to be heard and seen? Whose interest was I really serving? The answer to these questions came in a moment of time, but the practical application has been a life-time walk and it still is. To all of these questions there is one and only one answer.

The answer to these questions can be summed up with one question and one answer. The question is: How do you do everything in these verses? The answer is: Death to Self.

Were you looking for some complicated answer that you would struggle with for weeks and months before understanding? Well, let me say, 'Death to Self,' is hard enough. Dying to self and serving in the interests of God is accomplished when we find our identity in Christ who is in us and practice our position in Christ where we remain hidden.

Chapter 5

DEATH TO SELF

Here is a part of scripture that I believe many Christians do not know or understand. I believe that most of the Church has failed to teach the concept of 'death to self' and to help the Church body to grow in it. I am not saying that this is true for all, but from my experience, it seems to be true for many.

Let me ask again a few questions. Have you personally or have you heard another who was leading an individual to Christ and having them pray the sinner's prayer say, "in time you will overcome your sin?" Why can't they overcome them now? Where does it say in the

Bible that in time the cross, the blood of Christ, and the Resurrection will begin to work for you? Where does it say in the Bible that in the meantime you must struggle and fight with sin? There is no verse or passage of scripture that declares this. This thinking is right out of the pit of hell. Again, the Church has bought into the psychology of today's world.

If the work of Christ Jesus cannot set me free in this moment, then how can it set me free in the next moment, or the next week, or the next month, or the next year? To say that in time God will set me free is to say that there is no power in the work of the cross. And to me, that is disbelief! Man will not go to hell because of sin, for Christ took care of man's sin problem on the cross. What man will go to hell for is his disbelief in the work of Christ Jesus.

So, what is 'DEATH TO SELF?' First, let us understand our death in Christ Jesus and then we will look at what 'death to self' is. What part of you and me was it that died in Christ? The Apostle Paul states in Romans 6:5-11: "For if we have become united with Him in the likeness of His death, certainly we shall be also in the likeness of His resurrection, knowing this, that our old self was crucified with Him, that our body of sin might be done away with, that we should no longer be slaves to sin; for he who has died is freed from sin. Now if we have died with Christ, we believe that we shall also live with Him, knowing that Christ, having been raised from the dead, is never to die again; death no longer is master over Him. For the death that He died, He died to sin, once for all; but the life that He lives, He lives to God. Even so consider yourselves to be dead to sin, but alive to God in Christ Jesus."

Let's look at the phrase, "our old self," for here we will discover what of ourselves was in Christ's death. Have you ever watched little children and noted how self-centered they are? Nobody has to teach or train a child to pursue his or her needs above the needs of others. How many times have we had to teach and train the opposite over and over again? Do you know of any parents who actually sit down and teach their child to throw a tantrum while they were in the store?

My wife and I have five wonderful grandchildren. We are the kind of grandparents who love their grandchildren and want them around us as much as possible. As I watched them, I discovered that no one was teaching my grandchildren how to be self-centered. It just came to them as if they were born that way. I

35

know it is hard to believe that my grandchildren could be so self-focused and not care about others, but they are. However, do you know what? So are we! Here we all are living on this planet focused on ourselves trying to get acceptance out of people and this world. And, like children, we're not concerned with the consequences to others, only that we feel good to ourselves. It is for this that Jesus Christ came into this world.

God knew that mankind whom He created and loved was in a great dilemma; if man was going to overcome his self-centeredness, he would have to undergo a radical change in nature. In the Old Testament God, through His prophet Ezekiel, began to speak of this radical change that He would bring into the life of man. These verses are thought of as part of the New Covenant that God would bring in with His Son, Christ Jesus.

"A new heart will I give you and a new spirit will I put within you, and I will take away the stony heart out of your flesh and give you a heart of flesh. And I will put My Spirit within you and cause you to walk in My statutes, and you shall heed My ordinances and do them." (Ezekiel 36: 26-27)

Do we understand that God was the first heart surgeon? It was He who did the first heart transplant, taking a stony heart out and replacing it with a heart of flesh. And, while He was doing the heart transplant, He was also removing our old spirit nature and giving us a new spirit. How and when did He do this? He did it when He went to the cross for you and I. Romans 5:8 says, "But God demonstrates His own love toward us, in that while we were yet sinners Christ died for us."

I like the way the Apostle Paul describes it in Philippians 2:5-8, "Have this attitude in yourselves which was also in Christ Jesus, who although He existed in the form of God, did not regard equality with God a thing to be grasped, but emptied Himself, taking the form of a bondservant, and being made in the likeness of men. And being found in appearance as a man, He humbled Himself by becoming obedient to the point of death, even death on a cross."

In this passage of scripture, I believe all of man's trouble can be resolved. This passage not only teaches how God gave us a new heart and a new spirit; it shows us how we can live no longer for our self-centeredness, but for the Lord Jesus Christ.

Chapter 6

A CHOICE TO BE MADE

Say with me: CHOICE! What is choice? Choice is a gift! The Lord Jesus Christ chose to empty Himself of equality with God the Father, chose to take the form of a bondservant, chose to be found in the appearance of you and me, and chose to humble Himself by becoming obedient to the point of death on a cross. Because of these choices, He brought to you and me an opportunity to make a CHOICE!

My middle son has his own consulting business. Before that, he worked for a children's home in Goshen, IN where children and young teenagers were often brought because of the trouble they were in or the difficulties they were having. He was a program director there and worked with the young people to help them through their troubles. One of the things he taught them was that they had no problems and that there were no problems at the home. There were only opportunities to make a right CHOICE!

Before Christ Jesus, man was incapable of making right choices. The only people who could make a right choice were those to whom the Spirit of God would rest upon. Because of one man's, Adam's, wrong choice, all were affected by the death he chose. Thus any choice we would make before Christ was out of our self-centeredness to satisfy our feeling good about ourselves. When Christ, the second Adam, came He made a choice which made it possible for all men to make a right choice. A good example of this is what the Lord taught me through my wife and sons.

In January, 1991, our oldest son was hit by a semi-truck at 55 mph. Our son had driven into the truck in the early hours of the morning. Before the accident, he had been drinking with some friends and he became angry. To get over his anger, he took the car and went for a country drive.

My wife and I were awakened by a friend of our youngest son who was standing by our bed and telling us that a policeman was at the front door. He said that David was in an accident and we were needed at the hospital. It was in this experience that the Lord started to teach me about choice. The story of David's accident and wonderful recovery is a story in and of itself. However, it is from this story and life experience that God taught me about choice. Every time my thoughts turned toward David, I had to choose to trust God for his physical, emotional and spiritual well-being; I could do nothing of myself to save him.

God continued to work after his physical healing was manifest. Our middle son, Michael, was a student at Taylor University. He was getting ready for a summer job in New York where he would be painting houses to make money for the fall classes. He knew that his brother David had wandered away from the Lord and was coming back through this accident. Michael thought it would be good to ask his brother David to join him; he might encourage him in his walk back to the Lord while each of them made some money for school. David was planning to go to a 'Youth With A Mission' school in the fall to strengthen his relationship with the Lord and he needed money for the school. Both of them were excited about the summer job and I believe both were looking forward to encouraging each other.

Somewhere in their conversation they had been talking about their youngest brother Jarrett. They knew he needed encouragement also. Michael and David thought together that they could help Jarrett and encourage him in his walk with the Lord. They asked if they could invite him along with them for the summer. Of course, I thought, Wow! So, my wife, Lin, and I had to take them to New York to start their summer jobs.

We were planning to have a great summer, Lin and I. But, three weeks into the summer job on a Sunday afternoon at 1:00 p.m., the phone rang and it was David. He was beside himself. He was shouting over the phone, "I don't care what you have to do or who you have to get, be it the police or the army, but whatever you do, get him out of here!" My heart was racing now and I was not sure what was happening, so I asked, "What's wrong?" David's reply was, "Jarrett!" Again, I asked, "What's he doing?" David's reply was, "He's drinking and drugging and running around with women. He's breaking all the rules."

I am praying now, 'Lord, what do I say to him?' Without realizing it, these words came out of my mouth: "David, why did you and Michael ask Jarrett to go to New York with you?" He said, "We wanted to show him Jesus." I replied, "So, how are you doing?" All of a sudden David said, "What do you mean?" These words came from my lips: "David, you're right; what Jarrett is doing is wrong, but when the wrongs of another cause us to behave in a negative way, then all they are doing is being a mirror that shows us ourselves." David said to me in response, "I'll have to think about that for a while. I'll call you back later." I told him that if things didn't get better, we would work it out to bring him home.

When I put the phone down, the Lord spoke the following words to me as clear as day: 'Dave, that's you with your wife Lin.' I said to the Lord, 'I don't understand. What do you mean?' The Lord said to me, 'This is what you do to Lin all the time. You say, 'If you wouldn't act like that, I wouldn't act like this,' or 'if you wouldn't say that, I wouldn't say this.' You are always blaming her for how you feel and how you act. She doesn't make you feel or act the way you do. She's just a mirror showing you what you are like while you are not liking what she is like. She is blaming you and you are blaming her.'

Right there, I began to cry. I immediately went to find Lin and began to ask her to forgive me for my self-centeredness. It was here that God started teaching me to do nothing from selfishness or empty conceit. From Philippians 2 came a principle that I have been teaching for over 15 years. No one makes or causes me to say or do what I do, but myself.

I've learned that what we say or do does not determine how we feel or think. I have been teaching people that we have four things that we can control. Those four things are: our own thoughts, our own attitudes, our own words, and our own actions or behaviors. Jesus gave us this power of CHOICE!

Every thought creates an attitude. With that attitude, we determine the words which we'll speak and the behaviors that we'll carry out. Someone or something may stimulate our emotions, but once it's in our minds, we determine our emotional thought responses. Scripture encourages us to have the same attitude that was in Christ Jesus. Another word for attitude is mindset. A mindset is simply what we choose to say or do after any given situation or circumstance that happens to us. It is simply our emotional response to how we have determined to express ourselves after an event.

Our response will demonstrate if we have taken on Jesus' attitude by emptying ourselves of ourselves, becoming humble and taking the form of a bondservant on the behalf of others. Our response will demonstrate if we have become obedient to the point of death to self so that Christ's interest might be lived out through our lives. The believer often fails to understand or recognize that the battle is never fleshly, but always spiritual. We cannot stop thoughts from entering our minds, but once they do enter, the Bible teaches us to take every thought captive: "For though we walk in the flesh, we do not war according to the flesh, for the weapons of our warfare are not of the flesh, but divinely powerful for the destruction of fortresses. We are destroying speculations and every lofty thing raised up against the knowledge of God, and we are taking every thought captive to the obedience of Christ." (II Corinthians 10:3-5)

How I choose to think determines how I choose to live! Everything that happens to me is only an opportunity to make a right choice. Do I choose to let the flesh live or do I choose to let Christ live in my place?

"Wait a second here!" you may ask. "I thought you said that I died in Christ?" I did, but that which died in Him was my flesh nature. That which I must deal with is my body of flesh. As some have put it, it is the deeds or patterns of the flesh that I must deal with. Christ took care of my old nature, but I must take care of the deeds of my flesh. My actions are my choice.

Chapter 7

DEATH TO THE DEEDS OF THE FLESH

Here's a part of scripture that I have struggled with for years, mainly because I was taught wrong. I don't believe that I was taught wrong intentionally, but simply because that is how someone else taught those whom I learned from. Let's start with a verse of scripture in Luke 9:23-24. Jesus says, "If anyone wishes to come after Me; let him deny himself, and take up his cross daily, and follow Me. For whoever wishes to save his life shall lose it, but whoever loses his life for My sake, he is the one who will save it." Jesus' words are not difficult to understand, but let's see if we can make it a little more clear about what He is asking us to do.

Jesus says, "If anyone wishes to come after Me, let him deny himself." What does Jesus mean by, "deny himself?" In the Greek, which is the language the text was originally written in, the word is arnenomai. It is an interesting word. It means to deny utterly, disown, abstain; separate or depart from. In other words, Jesus is stating that the person who would follow Him must utterly disown, abstain, separate and depart from himself. What was it that Jesus died for on the cross? Was it not for the body of sin that it might be done away with? Romans 8:10 says, "For the death that He died, He died to sin, once for all; but the life that He lives, He lives to God." This is a spiritual truth that manifests itself in the physical lifestyle of the true believer.

Romans 8:11 says, "Even so consider yourselves to be dead to sin, but alive to God in Christ Jesus." There is a dimension of this truth that is a spiritual reality and one that has a physical application for living. In Romans 8:12-13 the scripture says, "So then, brethren, we are under obligation, not to the flesh, to live according to the flesh - for if you are living according to the flesh, you must die; but if by the Spirit you are putting to death the deeds of the body, you will live." Here is where many struggle with the Christian walk. Many feel and believe that it is impossible to deny the body of deeds. How does someone deny something that they carry around all day long?

Again, it is about one's CHOICE! There are many who teach and say that we are bound to sin and they claim Paul's teaching in Romans 7 as their proof. Many believe that Paul had this continual struggle with his flesh versus his spirit. I personally do not believe that Paul is claiming this as his way of life. I believe the individual's struggle occurs only if he or she does not make a choice to die to the deeds of the flesh.

First we need to understand what Paul is saying in verses 14-20, "For we know that the Law is spiritual; but I am of flesh, sold into bondage to sin. For that which I am doing, I do not understand; for I am not practicing what I would like to do, but I am doing the very thing I hate."

Let's stop for just a moment and look at a couple of the words. In verse 14 it says, "the Law is spiritual." The walking out of a spiritual exercise cannot be carried out without some divine intervention on the behalf of the one choosing to walk it out. Are we not one with Christ as we discovered in Colossians 3:3-4?

What about II Peter 1:3-11? Doesn't Peter write in verses 3-4, "Seeing that His divine power has granted to us everything pertaining to life and godliness, through the true knowledge of Him who called us by His own glory and excellence. For by these He has granted to us His precious and magnificent promises, in order that by them you might become partakers of the divine nature, having escaped the corruption that is in the world by lust."

When does one escape the corruption that is in the world by lust? Here it says we have already escaped the corruption. It is not something that is going to happen, but something that has already happened. That is why Peter writes in verse 5, "Now for this very reason also, applying all diligence, in your faith supply moral excellence, and in your moral excellence, knowledge; and in your knowledge, self-control, and in your self-control, perseverance, and in your perseverance, godliness, and in your godliness, brotherly kindness, and in your brotherly kindness, love." Do we apply all diligence or does God? And where is this diligence applied? You're right! We, as believers are to apply all diligence and we apply it with our faith.

Faith in what, you ask? All diligence is applied in the belief that what God says, He means and what He means, He says. By His divine power, He has granted to us everything we need for living and godliness for we are partakers of His divine nature and we can escape the corruption that is in the world by lust. Now this leads me to our second word, which is practice.

Looking at Romans 7:14, Paul uses the phrase, "for I am not practicing what I would like to do." But in II Peter 1:10, Peter says, "for as long as you practice these things, you will never stumble or fall." This is the key to dying to the flesh. We must practice putting to death the deeds of the flesh. Again, here is another truth we must discover. Just what is it that I must practice? I must practice staying in my position.

Watch what Paul goes on to say in Romans 7:24-25, "Wretched man that I am! Who will free me from the body of this death?" Paul is not talking about when he physically dies and goes to heaven. He is referring to the now, while he is still living in this tent of his body. He says, "Thanks be to God through Jesus Christ our Lord?"

He is declaring that he is free from the power of sin and death and that he does not have to sin. For him to be able to do this, he must claim his position in Christ Jesus. Listen to Romans 8:1-2, "There is therefore now no condemnation for those who are in Christ Jesus." Where is there no condemnation? You're right! In Christ Jesus there is no condemnation. Why? "For the law of the Spirit of life in Christ Jesus has set you free from the law of sin and death." Sin, honestly, has no power over anyone who practices his or her position in Christ and knows his or her identity in Christ Jesus.

Chapter 8

PHYSICAL LAW vs. SPIRITUAL LAW

Dr. Bill Bright says in his booklet, <u>Four Spiritual Laws</u>, "Just as there are physical laws that govern the physical universe, so are there spiritual laws that govern your relationship with God." We understand the law of gravity that says what goes up must come down. That is a physical law. One way that we can override the law of gravity is through the law of aerodynamics. When we are in an airplane, we can override the law of gravity by the law of aerodynamics.

Using this illustration, we apply this same thought to the law of sin and death. By being in Christ Jesus, we are able to overcome the law of sin and death through the law of the Spirit of life in Christ Jesus. If we are on our way to Jamaica for a vacation and the stewardess says, 'Dave, we just flew over Jamaica and we've pushed your luggage out on our first pass over. On our second pass, when you see the red light over the door turn on, you can jump and you'll be in Jamaica in just a few moments after you leave the airplane.'

Should I be so foolish as to follow those directions, what law would take effect on my life? Your right! The law of gravity would take over as soon as I left the airplane. So, for me to safely reach Jamaica for my vacation, I must remain in the plane until it lands. This principle works the same way with the spiritual laws.

For me to overcome the law of sin and death, I must remain in the law of the Spirit of life in Christ Jesus. It is only here that the law of sin and death has no effect on me. I must remain in Christ Jesus! He is my identity and my position. It is this truth that much of the Church has failed to teach and encourage those who would follow Jesus, that sin has no effect on you as long as you remain in Him. Someone may ask how this is possible, to remain in Jesus at all times?

If this were impossible, why would the Bible encourage us to "walk by the Spirit, and you will not carry out the desires of the flesh?" (Galatians 5:16) Why would the Bible say to "put on the Lord Jesus Christ, and make no provisions for the flesh in regard to its lusts." (Romans 13:14) If we were to put the Lord Jesus Christ on, where would we be and where would He be?

It's kind of like the law of dress. When I put a shirt on, I'm on the inside and the shirt is on the outside. Instead of myself being seen, I now let my shirt be seen. It is the same with Christ. Put on the Lord Jesus and you let Him be seen. Yet, someone else will say, 'How do I do this all the time?' The answer is in our eternal moment of now.

Chapter 9

LIVING ONLY IN THE MOMENT

Living only in the moment is another truth that we fail to teach. Jesus said in Matthew 5:34, "So do not worry about tomorrow; for tomorrow will care for itself. Each day has enough trouble of its own." James says, "Come now, you who say, 'Today or tomorrow we will go to such and such a city, and spend a year there and engage in business and make a profit.' Yet you do not know what your life will be like tomorrow. You are just a vapor that appears for a little while and then vanishes away." (James 4:13-14) Millions of believers are living tomorrow before they live today! We need to live in the moment.

It is a lie to tell someone that in time they will overcome or in time they will be victorious. Helping someone live in the moment can be one of the best encouragements that we can offer them. Jesus encourages us to live today before we live tomorrow. How much of today is lost to the fears and worries of tomorrow? Much or even most of it never happens anyways, or at least in the way we thought it would or imagined it to be. James says it just as strong as Jesus does, "Yet you do not know what your life will be like tomorrow. You are just a vapor that appears for a little while and then vanishes away." (James 4:14) We need to stay focused on what is and not on what may never be.

Jesus says in John 8:31-32, "If you continue in My word, then you are truly disciples of Mine." Let's stop here and look at the phrase, "If you continue in My word." To continue means to abide. So, what is Jesus actually saying? Jesus is saying that if we stay in His word, if we are present in His word and if His word is present in us, if we endure in His word, if we tarry in His word, we are truly His disciples. All of these ifs pertain to the present moment. Then He goes on and says, "and you will know the truth, and the truth will make you free." That freedom is ours now.

Here again is another phrase that we need to consider... "and you will know the truth." Jesus is not talking about intellectual knowledge by itself, but experiential knowledge as well. In other words, freedom comes from obeying the truth, not just knowing the truth. How many people have knowledge of the truth, but they don't practice the truth? Jesus is saying that His true disciples are those who continue in His word and obey and practice His word. These are the ones whom the truth will set free.

Jesus makes another statement in John 7:17, "If any man is willing to do His will, he shall know of the teaching, whether it is of God, or whether I speak from myself." Our answer to freedom is found in the phrase "If any man is willing to do His will." Until we stop living for ourselves, we'll never stop blaming others and God for not being able to overcome our struggles.

Again, who are we living for? Our answer reveals our position and our identity. Outside of Christ, we are bound to sin. But as we acknowledge our death in Christ, remain hidden in Christ and allow Christ to live through us, we overcome sin. Living in the moment of the reality of our position and identity in Christ is a truth that Paul was teaching when he said to the Ephesians, "therefore be careful how you walk, not as unwise men but as wise, making the most of your time, because the days are evil." (Ephesians 5:15)

Every day is a day filled with opportunities to die to self and let Christ live in our place. Even though I awake in this earth suit of mine, life is no longer about the earth suit. It is about what's in the earth suit, my new heart and my new spirit. One great reason why many in the Christian community are still hanging on to their hurts, pains, and hang-ups is because they are still focusing on their earth suit. When we encourage those who are in Christ to continue to focus on their outer man, we are in opposition to the Word of God.

The scripture says, "For those who are according to the flesh set their minds on the things of the flesh, but those who are according to Spirit, the things of the Spirit. The mind set on the flesh is death, but the mind set on the Spirit is life and peace, because the mind set on the flesh is hostile toward God, for it is not even able to do so, and those who are in the flesh cannot please God." (Romans 8:5-8)

Moment by moment living is a truth and teaching that encourages believers to die to the flesh and live by the Spirit in the present moment. For any hope given to, or life lived in the flesh will always be hostile toward God and death towards the individual. This brings a question to mind: When does one begin to start acting on his or her cry of repentance? Does it start "in time" or "now?" You're right! It starts now! It is right now that you and I have all the enabling grace of God that is needed to overcome any and every sin that has or would or could befall us.

Repentance is a truth that many in the body of Christ are not familiar with today. There are those who teach that we need to change our terminology for the modern minds if they are to understand the Bible. That is because many of us have forgotten that the Bible was not written to the mind of flesh, but to the Spirit of the man, the Spirit he would receive in Christ Jesus. (I Corinthians 2:1-16)

The Greek word metanoeo, is translated as repentance in the New Testament. It means "to think differently about something or to have a change of mind." Some may think, 'We thought you said that Christ Jesus has given us a new heart and a new spirit.'

He has, but the renewing or transforming of our minds is our responsibility. Scripture again says, "And that you be renewed in the spirit of your mind, and put on the new self, which in the likeness of God has been created in righteousness and holiness of the truth." (Ephesians 4:23, 24)

The scripture is teaching us that in Christ Jesus, we have already been created in righteousness and holiness of truth. This is something that is not going to happen, but it is something that has already been done. It is my responsibility to take this truth and begin to practice it. How do I do this, you ask? It is done by the building of this revealed truth of who I am in Christ Jesus.

You see, that is what the words renew and transform mean in the Greek language. They are construction terms for building something. How do we do that? Again, by obedience, we do what the scripture encourages us to do. "We are destroying speculations and every lofty thing raised up against the knowledge of God, and we are taking every thought captive to the obedience of Christ." (I Corinthians 10:5) Everything begins with a thought and from that thought, we build a mindset and from that mindset, we begin to form words and behaviors of what we believe about ourselves and our situations or circumstances that surround us. Every day is filled with events or happenings that are filled with opportunities to live for the flesh or live in and by the Spirit. Every day is about living to die and dying to live.

True repentance is actually this: it is changing my way of thinking and my way of behaving in any moment and every moment given to me, so that Christ can live in my place. Because of the love of God around my life, in my life, and through my life, I am as free as I'll ever be, now <u>and</u> tomorrow. If we cannot be free from the power of sin in this moment then there will be no freedom from sin in the next. If we cannot overcome any habitual pattern of behavior in this moment then we will not overcome it in time either. If we learn to live in the moment of time which has been given to us, being victorious in this moment, then surely the grace that empowers us in this moment will empower us to live victorious in the next. I'm not talking about the notion that says once saved always saved. What I'm talking about is a part of God's unmerited favor that has been ignored by many in the Christian community. That is God's enabling grace!

Chapter 10

GRACE TO CHANGE

The gospel of Jesus Christ never asks us to meet His requirements on our own. Grace is God's unmerited favor, given to a people who can neither earn nor deserve it. It is a gift. If we know that, why do we keep treating this wonderful gift as if it is worthless and of no value other than when we need it to excuse ourselves from our continual sinful behaviors?

The answer can be found in that many do not know about the second half of this wonderful grace. God has made it possible for every one of His children to experience this incredible resource of grace that allows them to live a godly life. It's not just His favor. It's about His enabling power that truly frees us to live according to His desires. It is not about wishing we could overcome or be free. It's not about wanting to do the right thing, but not being able to. It's not about, 'well, God knows my heart.' It's not about 'once saved always saved.' There is no scripture that says once you're in Christ Jesus, you will be saved, but you will not have the power to stop sinning. Nor is it about, 'well, I can't help myself because I still have this body of flesh with me.' No! Do we really believe that God would send His only begotten Son to die for the sins of the world and not make it possible for those He died for to walk and live in victory? Only those who would want to continue in the flesh and keep control over their lives would believe something like that.

It is not about the body. The body is only that which houses the spirit of the man. Christ died and put to death the old-man; He put to death our sin nature. Through our new birth in Christ, we receive a new heart and a new spirit. As Christ put to death the old-man or sinful nature, we are called to put to death the deeds of that old man or what we may see as our old patterns of behaving.

Many believers act as if they're obligated to sin because they still carry around this earth suit. But the scripture teaches, "So then, brethren, we are under obligation, not to the flesh, to live according to the flesh-for if you are living according to the flesh, you must die; but if by the Spirit you are putting to death the deeds of the body, you will live. For all who are being led by the Spirit of God, these are sons of God." (Romans 8:12-14)

Here again, we are talking about the enabling or empowering grace that is given to every believer to make a choice. This is not done based on the emotions of the flesh, but it is done according to faith and obedience to the Word of God. Do we believe our feelings or do we believe the Word of God? The Bible says that Christ is our life; that we are hidden with Christ in God. (Colossians 3:3) Verse 4 states, "When Christ, who is our life, is revealed, then you also will be revealed with Him in glory." Now, if Christ is our life and we are hidden with Christ in God, then who is to be seen? You're right! Christ is to be seen! We are hidden and are not to be seen until He returns. "When Christ, who is our life is revealed, then you also will be revealed with Him in glory." (Colossians 3:4)

Let's stop and take a look at this verse for a moment. Look at the phrase, "is revealed, then you also will be revealed with Him in glory." The phrase, "is revealed," is referring to the return of Christ, His second coming. But the phrase, "then you also will be revealed with Him in glory" is talking about you and I. So, here we are on planet earth and we are being asked to remain in position until the return of Christ, our position in Christ, who has become our identity.

That is why the scripture can go on and say, "Therefore consider the members of your earthly body as dead to immorality, impurity, passion, evil desire, and greed... put them all aside: anger, wrath, malice, slander, and abusive speech from your mouth. Do not lie to one another, since you laid aside the old self with its evil practices, and have put on the new self..." (Colossians 3:5-11)

All of this comes through the empowering grace of God. Grace allows us to do in the Spirit what we could not do in the flesh. Grace is not just God's unmerited favor; it is also an enabling force that empowers us to do works of righteousness that become the events and the proof of our salvation.

It's been illustrated this way: If your son or daughter were killed through some random act of violence and you, the father or mother, tracked down the guilty person and killed him, we would call that vengeance. Yet, if you, being the parent, called the police and the murderer was arrested, tried, convicted, and executed, we would call that justice. But at the trial you, being the parent of the child who was killed, plead for the guilty man's life to be spared and the judge and jury consented, we would call that mercy.

But what about this picture? In addition to pleading for the guilty one to be spared, you actually appeal to the judge to release the offender into your custody and care. Miraculously being given the approval, you take this man into your heart and home. You adopt him and raise him and love him as your own son... that would be grace!

Grace that not only forgives but grace that empowers is what we have in Christ Jesus. John Bevere in his book, Extraordinary: The Life You're Meant to Live, states, "Grace is a dynamic force that does more than affect our standing with God by crediting us with righteousness. Grace affects our experience as well."

Grace is a way of life. We must be utterly dependent on God's grace to live the Christian life. How can anyone live 24/7 without sinning? How can anyone live every day without remembering the hurts, pains, and hang-ups that have so easily entangled them? Only by GRACE!

Chapter 11

GRACE EMPOWERS BY OBEDIENCE

As a parent, can you imagine letting your child live by partial obedience? When you set a rule or standard for your children to obey, do you want partial obedience or full and complete obedience? Being a parent and a grandparent myself, I can't believe that you don't want full and complete obedience. Yet, how many within the Christian life feel that full and complete obedience is impossible? C. S. Lewis wrote, "I was not born to be free, I was born to adore and to obey." Obedience is foundational to the Christian life.

There is only one sin for which a person will go to hell. That is the sin of disbelief which results in our acts of disobedience. Disobedience is an action that shows forth our lack of faith and trust in God. It is we, ourselves, who are declaring ourselves to be God in this moment. We're also declaring the absence of His presence in this moment. We don't consciously or even verbally state this about ourselves however we just act as if it is so. To act in this way is to say, 'It is so.'

Have you ever heard the statement, 'more is caught than taught?' Our actions always have a greater impact than our words. This makes the declaration, 'Do as I say, not as I do' sound really foolish, doesn't it? God expects His followers not only to do what He says, but also what He does. This is why He has given us grace. The power of grace is found in our obedience not in our acknowledgement alone.

There is a power in grace that is released when acts of obedience are expressed. In Ephesians 5:1-2, we are encouraged, "Therefore be imitators of God, as beloved children; and walk in love, just as Christ also loved you and gave Himself up for us, an offering and a sacrifice to God as a fragrant aroma." We are asked to be imitators of God. If it were impossible, why then would we be encouraged to do so? I believe it is about our choice: to live through the body of flesh or to live through the Spirit.

The Bible teaches us that God's grace is undeserved, but it is not unconditional. Grace is available to everyone who would but receive it, but it is given only to the humble of heart. (James 4:6) It is our acts of obedience that release this empowering grace. God resists (literally, sets Himself against) those who are self-sufficient; those who try to manage their lives without Him. He resists all who would struggle and strive to live the Christian life on their own. These are those who are too full of pride to acknowledge their need of Him. This too is playing God!

Let's ask ourselves a question here. What is it that gives grace or makes grace an empowering force? I believe that scripture is clear on this point. In Acts 1:8, we find Jesus speaking about the promise of the Holy Spirit. Let's listen to His statement about the Spirit and what would happen when He would be poured out on men. "But you will receive power when the Holy Spirit has come upon you; and you shall be My witnesses both in Jerusalem, and in all Judea and Samaria, and even to the remotest part of the earth."

Let me ask a personal question here. What kingdom are you giving witness to? I believe that your answer to this question will show forth what power you are trying to live under or by. Jesus says that we would "receive power when the Holy Spirit comes upon" us. (Acts 1:8) What kind of power is He talking about? It is the power to be witnesses. The words "to be" are most important here. It's not about doing witnessing. It is about being a witness. Listen to Acts 4:13, "Now as they observed the confidence of Peter and John and understood that they were uneducated and untrained men, they were amazed, and began to recognize them as having been with Jesus." Now this is enabling grace in action. It is not just unmerited favor, but the power 'to be' from the Holy Spirit.

Some may say that it takes time to become or to be, that it just doesn't happen overnight, that it takes time to overcome. It does not take time if all that I have is this present moment. Living within the moment is living within the presence of the Eternal, and if He who is Eternal has given to me His Holy Spirit, then all I need is already mine in the Spirit. I am called to give witness to the power of Christ only in the present moment for I do not have a tomorrow as of yet. Should I receive a

71

tomorrow, I have 'to be' only in that moment by the power of the Spirit, by God's enabling grace.

It is my obedience that releases Gods enabling grace, the Holy Spirit's power. What is it that I am being a witness to? By my act of obedience, I am showing forth a transformed life that has been with Jesus Christ. This act of obedience gives demonstration to my faith which says that I no longer live by the law of sin and death but by the law of the Spirit of life in Christ Jesus. It demonstrates that I am free from sin's power over my life.

The law of the Spirit of life in Christ Jesus is not for yesterday. Yesterday is gone and I cannot change it. Nor is the law of the Spirit of life in Christ Jesus for tomorrow; for I do not yet have tomorrow and may never see it. All that I have is this moment. The scripture says that the law of the Spirit of life in Christ Jesus has set me free. Where? It has set me free right here in this very moment of time. All that happens to me in this moment of time is an opportunity to make a right choice by the enabling grace of the Holy Spirit that gives full expression to the transforming work of God in my life. We now can live a righteous and holy life that is complete, not one that is going to be complete, but is complete already at this moment in time.

Chapter 12

LIVING A LIFE THAT IS COMPLETE

It's hard to believe that we are complete, but scripture declares this to be true. Listen to this verse of scripture: "For in Him all the fullness of Deity dwells in bodily form, and in Him you have been made complete, and He is the head over all rule and authority." (Colossians 2:9, 10) Let's ask ourselves another question here. Where is it that we are made complete? Did you hear what the scripture said? In Him, we are made complete!

I know that the scripture also teaches, "that He who began a good work in you will perfect it until the day of Christ Jesus." (Philippians 1:6) God is not asking us to be something that we are not; God is asking us to be something that we are already. We are in Him and in Him we are the righteousness and the holiness of God in Christ Jesus. To be what we are in Christ, we must believe what the Bible says about us in Him. Let us always remember that Christ is eternal. He is eternal life. It is not something that we are going to, but something that we have already entered into, in Him.

Think of it like this: eternal is present. Present equals presence! We are always in His eternal presence for He is eternally present. Now, there are only three ways in which we can be out of His presence. First, until a person acknowledges Christ Jesus as the only way into the Father's presence, we are separated from God. John 14:6 says so clearly for us, "Jesus said to him, 'I am the way, and the truth, and the life; no one comes to the Father but through Me." Jesus said that it is through Him that we get to the Father. Outside of Christ there is no presence. There is only frustration and confusion along with broken and lost lives.

Second, if we are believers and step back into yesterday, what have we done? We've stepped out of His presence. This is often what many believers do. They are caught up in yesterday. Is there anyone that you have known who has been able to change the past? Yet, hundreds of believers are filling our churches still focused on the past. They are unable to do anything about their hurts, their pains, and their hang-ups. They find that Christ is not able to help them. Why is that? It is because they are living in their past and He is living in their present.

This brings us to the third reason. How many of us are living tomorrow before we live today? Two enemies of the body of Christ that we do not recognize are yesterday and tomorrow. God is eternally present. For any believer to live in yesterday or tomorrow is to step out of the presence of God. We must be present to know and experience His power that sets us free from the power of sin and death. There is no life outside of Christ, only death and a state of feeling lost.

Many believe it is impossible to live every moment of every day in Christ. I say to those who believe this way that they live their lives in unbelief. And, it is unbelief that will keep a person from stepping into the kingdom of God. Many who are ministering today are focusing on the outer man of the individual. I believe their focus must be turned to the inner man of who they are in Christ Jesus.

Listen to Paul's prayer in I Thessalonians 5:23-24: "Now may the God of peace Himself sanctify you entirely; and may your spirit and soul and body be preserved complete, without blame at the coming of our Lord Jesus Christ. Faithful is He who calls you, and He also will bring it to pass." Paul shares with us the order we need to be focusing on as we help and encourage ourselves and those who are hurting and struggling with the issues of life.

We must start with the spirit of the person and then the soul (mind and emotions) and finally the body. We need to see the spiritual beings that we are in Christ, helping every believer to come to know their identity and their position first. As we grow into that understanding, begin to practice our identity and take our position in Christ, everything else will follow. If we believe that life is about the earth suit or the outer-man, then we will continue to minister and serve the same people over and over again; we will never see them being set free from the power of sin and death.

John writes in I John 3:5, 8b, "You know that He appeared in order to take away sins; and in Him there is no sin... The Son of God appeared for this purpose, to destroy the works of the devil." Did you take note what the scripture said? "And in Him there is no sin." Where is the believer? You're right! The believer is in Him and in Him there is no sin. WOW! Praise God that every believer can be free from the power of sin and death. But our freedom is dependent upon our willingness to be in Him.

How about you? Are you living in your identity and have you taken your position in Christ? It all begins with making a choice to die to self and letting Christ live in your place. Can I encourage you, my friend, to make that decision right now, in Jesus' name?

Our biggest battle is neither sin nor the devil, for Christ defeated them both for us. Our biggest battle is in believing what the Bible says about us being in Him. For our flesh is in conflict with our spirit and it is here that we battle to live and walk by the Spirit and not the flesh. When we choose to die to the flesh, it is then that we will live and the truth of His word will set us free from the hurts, the pains, and the hang-ups of our lives.

Chapter 13

DIVINE FOCUS

Moving into our position and claiming our identity "in Christ" is one of the greatest challenges we'll ever have as believers. So how do we do it? We do it by "Divine Focus." Every believer is called to follow the example set for them by the Author and Perfecter of our faith, Jesus Christ. (I Peter 2:21; Hebrews 12:2)

Let's ask ourselves another question: Do we have an earthy mind-set or a heavenly mind-set? As believers and followers of Jesus Christ we must be focused on things above. In the book of Colossians 3:1-2 it says to us, "Therefore if you have been raised up with Christ, keep seeking the things above, where Christ is, seated at the right hand of God."

Before going any farther let's listen to what this verse is encouraging us to do. First, it is declaring our position "in Christ." Second, it is stating that we are to "keep seeking the things above." Verse 2 of this chapter tells us, "Set your mind on the things above, not on the things that are on earth." This verse is just restating verse one and truly encouraging a heavenly mind-set.

I know that some good and meaningful person is going to make the statement we've all heard over the years... that a person should not be so heavenly minded that they do no earthly good. This is one of those quotes that seems like good advice but when truly focused upon makes no heavenly sense.

Let me be a little bold here and say we're not called to do earthly good. Jesus didn't come to do earthly good; He came to do heavenly good. Earthly good is temporal and Heavenly good is eternal. Let's listen to Jesus' proclamation of Himself in John 3:10-12, "Jesus answered and said to him, 'Are you the teacher of Israel and do not understand these things? Truly, truly, I say to you, we speak of what we know and testify of what we have seen, and you do not accept our testimony. If I told you earthly things and you do not believe, how will you believe if I tell you heavenly things?" Again in John

7:16-17, "... My teaching is not Mine, but His who sent Me. If anyone is willing to do His will, he will know of the teaching, whether it is God or whether I speak from Myself." Also in John 8:28-30, "...When you lift up the Son of Man, then you will know that I am He, and I do nothing on My own initiative, but I speak as the Father taught Me. And He who sent Me is with Me; He has not left Me alone, for I always do the things that are pleasing to Him." Jesus had a heavenly mind-set, while fulfilling His Divine Calling and Purpose on earth.

I have read a statement by Pastor Rick Warren that speaks to us here, "There is nothing quite as potent as a focused life, one lived on purpose. The men and women who have made the greatest difference in history were the most focused." Jesus is the greatest example of all!

How could Jesus be so focused? First, He always remained in His Position and always declared His Identity, "I and the Father are One." Only heavenly good could break the power of sin and death and only One who had a heavenly mind-set could defeat the enemy of our soul. Now the choice is ours; will we see the hurts, the pain, and the hang-ups as opposition or as opportunity for our Divine calling and purpose to follow in His steps? (Philippians 2:3-11; I Peter 2: 21-25; 4:1-4)

Make a choice right now by first asking Christ to forgive you of your sins and become your Savior and the Lord of your life.   After you have done that, start declaring Him as your Position and your Identity, knowing that you now have Divine Focus to carry out your calling and purpose for the Kingdom of God. Blessing's to you as you let Christ live in your place, for we who follow Christ are Dying to Live!

BIBLIOGRAPHY

NEW AMERICAN STANDARD BIBLE; Zondervan: copyright 2002

Seeking Him; Nancy Leigh DeMoss and Tim Grissom: Moody Publishers Chicago

Lifetime Guarantee; Bill Gillham: Harvest House Publishers Eugene, Oregon 97402

Getting Healthy Again; Rick Warren: PURPOSE DRIVEN PREACHING: Sermon Audios and Transcripts on Compact Disc- 2004